My Name is Mary

A Memoir of a 96-Year-Old Woman Who Found Supreme Love and Happiness

Mary Ivy Fox

Copyright © 2017 by Mary Fox

Los Angeles, California
All rights reserved
Printed and Bound in the United States of America

Professional Publishing House
1425 W. Manchester Ave. Ste. B
Los Angeles, California 90047
323-750-3592
Email: professionalpublishinghouse@yahoo.com
www.Professionalpublishinghouse.com

Cover design: TWA Solutions
First Printing: November 2017
978-0-9983089-7-5
10987654321

No part of this book may be reproduced, stored in a retrieval system or transmitted in any form or by any means without the prior written permission of the publisher—except by a reviewer who may quote brief passages in a review to be printed in a newspaper, magazine or journal. For inquiries contact the publisher.

Dedication

This book is dedicated to my late mother, Everline Benson Scherrer, who taught us to be clean and "to do the job right."

Acknowledgments and Thanks

First, I want to thank my husband, Dr. Logan Fox, for helping me put this little book together, Dr. Rosie Milligan, for taking our hand-written manuscript and turning it into a book, and a host of friends who pushed me to write.

Chapter 1

My Name is Mary Ellen Sherrer

I was born on May 1, 1921, the fifth child born to Ben and Everline Sherrer. I was born in the small town of Rayle, Georgia. As a baby, I was said to be cute with a little round face with dimples. In fact, my mother was told by a neighbor that another neighbor had planned to kidnap me.

My sisters, Nancy and Laura and brother, Willie, were older than I. One sister died as a baby at one month old. My sister, Julia, was three years younger and a brother, Sam, was born when I was eleven years old. The family soon moved to the town of

Washington where I started school in a one-room school house.

When I was about seven or eight years old, I would talk back to my mother, something that children of that time were not supposed to do. As a Taurus or Bull, I just could not stop until my mother used the rod on me. When I was about nine, my father's sister came to visit us and carried me home with her. She had two daughters and two sons. There wasn't much food in the house as she worked only a few days a week, but there were a lot of men coming and in out of the house. I was not happy with the things that I saw and I cried day and night. My aunt called my father and he came and got me.

After being home with the family, another aunt came for a visit and took me home with her. She had one son and a niece living with her. I was able to go to school there, but the son mistreated me, and I finally went back home to be with my mother and sisters, Julia and Laura, and my brother, Sam. It was a good time and all was going well.

Then one day an uncle came to visit. He asked my mother if he could take me home to Atlanta with him. He promised her that I could attend school, which seemed to persuade my mother and she agreed. I was about thirteen or fourteen and I went with him.

Actually, he did not live in the city, but in a small town called Carey Park. He lived in a two-room house. At the time, his wife had left him. They had one child, Christine, who was about seven years old. It turned out that what he really wanted was a maid. I had everything to do, take care of Christine, cook, wash and mop the floors. This uncle also had pigs, which would get out of the pen, then I had to run them down and get them back in their pen.

I did go to Washington High School and liked it. I made good grades.

One day, my uncle's wife came back to him, and after all I had done taking care of her daughter, she told my uncle to send me back home. She wanted to get me out of the house. When he didn't do so, she told me I should marry an old man who she said really liked me, but I was not going to marry that old man.

So, one morning, she did not go to work and told me to hurry to school. I knew that she was not into my going to school. I went to school and when I came back home, to my surprise, she had left. All my things were on the floor, and she had left the key next door. One of the ladies in the neighborhood came to me and put her arm around me.

Before the wife came back, I had done everything I could to find a job working after school. I got a job at a Drive-In, making $3.50 a week. The people who owned the Drive-In had two places, one of which was a night club across the river. The wife ran the Drive-In and the husband ran the Night Club.

One day, the husband came to the Drive-In when I was working and told his wife he needed me to clean the Night Club. I had a feeling this was not true, so I prepared myself for what I felt was coming. I was right; he tried to rape me. I had to fight him off, praying to God for help. Finally, he gave up and took me back to the Drive-In. God was with me as this man could have dropped me in the river.

Making $3.50 a week, I was saving my money as I liked nice clothes, but one day, my uncle asked me for the money I had saved. Unfortunately, he never gave it back.

After I was thrown out of my uncle's house, I got in touch with my sister. I waited until she came home from work and told her what had happened. Laura told me that she and I could get a place together. She told me I would have to get a job. I was in the 10th grade. I went and told my homeroom teacher that I had to quit school and get a job to support myself and she had compassion on me.

Laura and I got a room. I got a job where Laura was working at a garment factory. The job was within walking distance from the room we had rented.

One day, a man came to the factory door looking for us. He told us the lady whom we paid our rent to, was being put out of the house, and our things would be put on the street. We immediately left the job and went to the house before our things were put out. It turned out, the lady we were renting from was not paying her rent, but giving the money to her boyfriend.

We were in shock with no place to go. We called our Aunt Carrie, hoping she might help us and she did. She told us to come to her house and stay with her. I stayed with her until I left Atlanta.

In 1941, World War II now involved America and I wanted to help my country. I was working at a place that made bottle tops and I was not happy with my job. I then went to City Hall where they posted government jobs. One day I found what I was looking for. The Army was looking for people to work at repairing airplane engines. I had to take a test, but I made a good score. I told Julia about the opportunity and she went and did the same thing. First, we had to be trained on machines. The school required us to be in class from midnight until morning. We were still working our old job so we got little sleep, but we were young and strong.

While living with Aunt Carrie, Laura and I went to a Baptist Church and after going for a while, we joined and I was baptized in a creek by Rev. Matthew.

During this time, Laura was on the wild side, she liked night clubbing, drinking with her friends, including her pastor and another minister.

One morning she asked me to stop by the pastor's place and return something that belonged to him. I agreed since he lived near where I was working. When I got there and knocked, he opened the door and tried to pull me in to rape me. I had to fight him off with all my strength. I won that fight, but I was shocked and never went back to that church. I never told Laura what had happened.

After a two-month's training at Clark College, we were sent to Mobile, Alabama where we had six more weeks of training before being put on the assembly line. We took apart engines of airplanes that had been shot down. The engines were cleaned and put back together again. Doing this work, we were called aircraft machinists.

At the time, it was hard to find a place to live in Mobile. We were forced to live with people who seemed to care only for the money they could make from people like us who came from out of town.

After we had been there for a while, the government built homes for us; our home included one bedroom, a kitchen, and a bath. It was clean, neat and near enough to where we our job was located so that we could walk to work. We were required to be on time. If we were late, money would be deducted from our paycheck.

One morning, a train had stopped across our path. There were several of us so we decided to crawl under the train, which we did and got to work on time.

My sister, Julia, was in Mobile, Alabama before me, because I had been under a doctor's care due to a smashed finger. When I was released from the doctor, I joined her in Mobile where I entered the training class. I was one of four in my group. At this time, there was a black woman over the school, but my instructor was a white Army Officer. When the class was finished, the ones that passed were given a certificate. When all the names of those who passed were called, my name was not among them.

The Army Officer went to this woman. "Why was Mary Sherrer's name not called?" he asked. "She was the best student in my class."

"Oh," the lady said. "I called her name, but she was probably talking and didn't hear me."

Of course, this was not true, but for some reason, this woman did not like me. I thanked my instructor for his intervention.

After I passed, I started working on the assembly line. There were two of us at one station. One time, we dropped an engine off the line. We had to have help to get it off the floor. Since we were working under the military, we had to go to personnel and see a Captain. He was nice about the situation. "It could have been worse," he said.

While working the swing shift, we would eat lunch outside. In Alabama, at night, the moon shone like day. We worked one month on the day shift and one month on swing shift. Because of this, we often missed our rations and were hungry a lot of the time.

On one particular night, there were five of us having lunch. Two other girls joined us. They had been to San Francisco and they told us how nice the young men had treated them there. They said the young men would bring candy and flowers when they came to see you.

So, five of us said, "Let's go to California." Eventually, we all did get to California. Julia came before I did. One of the girls had been to Los Angeles, so that's where they came. This girl knew a family living in Los Angeles who set them up until they could find a place. The only place one could get was a room in someone's home.

Julia's friend, Miriam, knew a family that had a room to rent and they got the room.

In July 1944, at age twenty-three, I came to Los Angeles. Before coming, I wanted to be sure I could keep my "Availability Card" for government work. I went to personnel and talked to the Captain. I told him I needed to go to Atlanta to care for my mother. He gave me the card and I thanked him.

I left Mobile and went to Atlanta to be with my mother. I asked her to understand what I wanted to do. She gave me her blessings and told me to go and be with Julia in Los Angeles.

I came to Los Angeles by train, going through Chicago and Salt Lake City. Military service people were the first to be served in the dining car. A soldier sat next to me and when I told him I was going to Los Angeles, he said that's where he was going, too. At meal time, he told me I could go with him. I did and I was served.

Getting to Los Angeles, I got a cab to take me to where Julia lived. She was happy to see me. After I arrived, the Landlady put a folding bed on the patio.

After living with Julia and Miriam, I noticed that they were buying food together, but Miriam had met this man who claimed he owned property and she would cook dinner for him in hopes of getting him. Of course, she used food that Julia had helped to pay for. I told Julia that we needed to get a place of our own. Shortly thereafter, we moved in with a couple with a little baby. They were nice and treated us like family.

Meantime, I went to the unemployment office to look for a job. I was asked where I had worked and I told the lady that I hadn't worked—that I was still in school. She sent me to a small factory, which made air tubes for airplanes. I worked there for a while, but I wanted to work for the government again.

I would go down to City Hall and check out the listing board for government jobs. One day I found what I was looking for. I filled out the application paper and gave the time I had worked for the government in Mobile. After several weeks, I was notified that I was accepted. I then received a letter telling me to come for an interview. The day I was to go was on a Friday when I had to be at the job I had then, but Julia was off that day. So, I asked her to go in and have the interview acting as if she was me. She went in and had the interview as Mary and it went well. She was told to hurry and get her picture taken before they closed for the day. She didn't dare do this so she killed time in the restroom. She made a map for me to follow so I could get my picture taken on Monday. I got my picture taken and went to work.

The job was in Maywood and, after a few days on the job, personnel found me a ride with a Mr. Simons who lived near me. So, I had a ride for the rest of the time I worked at Aircraft Command.

As I mentioned earlier, we were living with this couple with the little baby. There was a woman living in the back who cooked for people. One of the people she cooked for was a man named James Edward King. He saw me and wanted to meet me. Hence, the lady said, she would cook him a meal and he could invite me to dinner. This is what happened. I met him. Afterwards, he asked me to dinner several times. He was a very neat man, fourteen years older than I was. I had been thinking that an older man could bring stability to me. Besides, my mother was urging me to get married, as she didn't like the idea of my being alone. So, I married King on March 15, 1945.

Chapter 2

My Name is Mary S. King

I called him King. He would drink every day, so much so at first that I asked him about it. He said, his father would give it to him. As time passed, his drinking became a serious problem. He started to hide his half pint of whiskey and he became mean.

I was trying to work for a better life, but he tried to discourage me, saying, "We will never have anything."

One day he came home and told me he had put a down payment on a house, saying, "It has a good foundation." He had not consulted me and I never did like the place, a duplex on Halldale Avenue. His drinking continued to get worse over time. Finally, he turned out to be a complete drunkard; by then, I had enough and asked for a divorce.

We had been married for fifteen years and had a five-year-old boy, Bruce. The court gave me Bruce and the house and gave King the car. The taxes were overdue, and I had to work extra hours to pay them off. I found a wonderful woman that kept children and she took care of Bruce. She had mostly boys and she was good with children, feeding them and even washing their clothes. I was so happy to have found her.

Bruce was five years old and started to school. The lady, Mrs. Ezell, had a husband who helped her with the children and he would take the children to school, which was not far from their home. Bruce was a good student.

Mrs. Ezell lived some distance from where I lived and since I had no car, I had to take him to Mrs. Ezell some way. Sometimes I would call a cab, but if I had the time I would use the bus, then I would take the bus to my job. Sometimes I would ask a neighbor to take us.

During this time, I was a mother, father, sister and brother to Bruce and responsible for providing a living for us. One day a neighbor asked me if I would be interested in buying a car. He had seen one on the parking lot of NBC Studio.

"Yes, I would like to buy a car!"

The price was $50.00 cash; So, I bought the car. I had earlier learned to drive with an automatic transmission, but now I had to learn to drive a stick shift. My brother gave me driving lessons, , but at least I had transportation.

Some other problems came along; someone would take parts off of the car, like the battery. To stop this, I put a hole in the hood and put a chain lock on the car. After driving this car for several years, I was able to buy another second-hand car.

I was working for a company that made neckties and not making much money. This company was in downtown Los Angeles in an old building on the second floor. There was a company called Adrian of California on the third floor. One day, Mr. Adrian Schenk asked my boss if I could come up to his place to help since his usual helper was on vacation. I started working for Adrian of California. This company would buy wholesale and resell to stores such as Grocers. The job I was assigned was packing and shipping to their stores. I learned fast and I liked this better than making ties. Mr. Schenk was surprised by my learning ability and asked me if I wanted to work for him. When I said, "Yes," the job was mine. The boss from the old job asked me if I wanted to stay on this new job. I told him I did. Then, he asked Mr. Schenk if he was going to keep me. He wanted to be sure I would have a job. I thanked him for that.

Mr. Schenk was the best boss I ever had. There were only three people working there. He told me that if we could do the job, the pay would be better. So, I really worked and I was making a good salary.

I met his wife, Phyllis, who was also a good person. I became like one of the family. They lived in Glendale as the company had moved there. Glendale was a city that did not like black people. The Civil Rights Movement had started. During this time, I was invited with my son to come to their home and spend the weekend. We went and stayed overnight. The next morning, we had breakfast out on the patio in full view of the neighbors.

Mr. Schenk said, "This is good for the neighbors. They need to know that black people are also people."

Saturday night the four of us went to a fine restaurant in Glendale. I had only a light jacket, so Phyllis put her mink coat on me. After dinner, as we were leaving, the doorman felt the coat and asked me who I was.

"I am Mrs. King and this is my son, Bruce."

His face turned red. I told Phyllis about this, and she called him a bastard.

I worked for Adrian for eighteen years. He was very good to me and I learned many good things from him.

One day a white man was unloading boxes of things we had ordered from his truck. He handed me the invoice and I started counting the boxes he had unloaded. He didn't say a word, but he went to the truck, opened the door, and brought out two more boxes he had left in the truck for himself. He hadn't figured on my counting the boxes to see if they matched the invoice. He said nothing, I told Mr. Schenk about this.

Mr. Schenk was born in Holland to American parents and he spoke several languages, He was an engineer, a graduate of Notre Dame. He had no sympathy for racial bigotry.

While working in Glendale, one day, I parked on the street about three feet from a driveway. When I went to get my car, this little white man came to me and said I had blocked his driveway. He was quite upset and probably thought I would get smart with him. To his surprise, I politely said to him, that I was very sorry if I had blocked his driveway. He was shocked, turned red and was speechless.

For my fiftieth birthday, my boss and his wife gave me a birthday party at their home. All the people of the company were invited as were some of my friends, including my sister Julia and her husband. I received some nice gifts and it was a very happy party.

One of the ladies in the office and Adrian were heavy smokers. The building stayed full of smoke. During his last years, Mr. Schenk developed cancer of the throat. He was a strong man and he kept working quite a while, even when he could hardly stand up. In time, he had to go to the hospital. He passed away in 1972.

I continued to work there until the business was sold. Then I worked for the buyer for a while, but he said, I was being paid too much, so he wanted me to train someone to take my place at a lower pay.

I had a friend working for a lock and key company. I asked him to bring me an application. I filled it out and turned it in. I was given a job making locks and keys. I worked there for ten years and retired in 1987; I am still getting a pension check in 2017.

Before retirement, I was at a yard party and met a man, Leroy Ivy. I called him Ivy. He had one son and I had one son. We had a brief courtship. He had his own home, was five years older than I, and it seemed to me that this would be a good relationship. He asked me to marry him and we were married, October 8, 1979. I moved into his house.

Chapter 3

My Name is Mary K. Ivy

Things went well for a while. Ivy had worked for United Airlines, but was then retired. I was still working at Wiser, the lock and key company; I worked on the swing shift. Ivy had worked for United for eighteen years and we could get passes to travel first class free—very nice! We did some traveling; Hawaii, St. Louis, Atlanta.

Ivy told me he was nervous. I thought that everybody got nervous, but his was different. His was a condition the doctor treated with pills and more pills, which were actually dope. I was enrolled in a Kaiser Health Insurance

Plan through my job and I got him in too. The doctor he was assigned to tried to get him off the pills. Because of this he suffered withdrawal symptoms, such as an inability to sleep. It was a very hard time for him, and he would continually tell me he was going to die. At times, he wanted to kill himself.

After retiring, I started to walk every morning for my health, mainly my mental health. I walked at Park Circle in the City of Inglewood. I got there at 6:00 a.m. and enjoyed walking with my friends. This was a good time for me and sometimes I would walk until 8:00 a.m. Ivy would still be in bed. He would get up and take his pills.

Walking every morning with my friends was a great help to me. I became the unofficial greeter to new people who joined us.

One day, in 1999, a new man started walking the circle. Somehow, he was different. He walked very fast, wearing a black beret. He would pass me and say, "Good morning." I was curious and wanted to know who he was.

One day, he stopped long enough to tell me he was Kenneth Hahn's brother-in-law. Kenneth Hahn was a well-known and well-liked Supervisor of L.A. County. He was a good man, was kind to black people, so of course, I knew of Kenneth Hahn. This man told me his name was Logan Fox and I told him my name. After that, we were friendly to each other.

Another morning, sometime later, he stopped and told me that he had sold his house. He was moving to San Pedro, a port city south of Los Angeles. I was sad to know he was leaving since I had started to really like this man. I asked him if he would come back to see us sometime. He took my phone number and said that after he was settled, he would come back and take me to see his place. There was a girl standing with me so he was talking about taking both of us to see his place.

Logan's wife had passed away in April, a little while before he began walking and my husband died in December 2000, after twenty-one years of marriage. Logan had been married fifty-six years.

Sure enough, after a few months, Logan came and picked up me and the other girl and took us to see his apartment. His place was full of flowers and when I asked him about them, he told me that he had planted them.

The other girl made a play for Logan, patting her hips and saying, "Look, Logan." She did this twice, once in the apartment, and once at the restaurant, where we went for lunch. This embarrassed me, but she really wasn't my friend, only someone who walked the circle. Logan didn't pay any attention to her.

Later, Logan asked me for a date. He picked me up and we returned to San Pedro, where we walked by the seashore, then met some friends. We had coffee and cookies at the corner store. I met his son, Logan Lee, who was an artistic painter. We went back to Logan's apartment where we got better acquainted, then went to breakfast at Caro's.

Our courtship had begun, April 9, 2002.

The next member of his family I met was his sister, Ramona. She was a wonderful person and was the wife of Kenneth Hahn.

The week after this first date, we went to the Getty Museum. Thereafter, every week we went to some interesting place. We went to the Forest Lawn Cemetery, the Huntington Library, Catalina Island, etc.

We began our courtship in April 2002. In October, we drove to Williams, Arizona to see the Grand Canyon. We were having Martinis in the Spencer Lounge of the hotel when Logan said, "Let's get married and worry about where we will live later."

"Yes," I said. He then urged me to have a church wedding since I had not had one before.

I have been a member of Trinity Baptist Church for many years, I knew I could do this. After getting home I called and made an appointment with my pastor, Reverend Alvin Tunstill. After I told him I had met a man walking, he said, "You are going to marry this man?"

I said, "Yes!"

I asked him not to make an announcement to the church since we wanted only our families and close friends to attend the ceremony and the reception. He promised, but immediately told the girls in the office. He told them they should start walking, because Mrs. Ivy met a husband-to-be doing so. They wanted to know where I walked, but I told them I had already taken the best of the men there (smile).

We planned the wedding for March 8, 2003. We decided that each of us could invite ninety people for a total of one hundred and eighty people. We had a very good service with family and friends. Logan's son, Logan Lee, was his best man. Christine Burleson was my maid of honor. I was escorted down the aisle on the arm of my son, Bruce, and my grandson, Chris; Chris's half-sister, Jasmine, was the flower girl.

At the wedding were his two daughters and his nephew and niece, Jimmy and Janice Hahn. Jimmy was the Mayor of Los Angeles and Janice was on the

City Council. Also, three of Logan's friends from Japan had come to be at the wedding.

At the reception we asked for the song, "Love is a Many Splendored Thing," to be played. We considered it "our song." On our date to the Getty Museum, which sits high on a hill, I asked Logan if he knew the song, "Love is a Many Splendored Thing." I was reminded of the words "high on a windy hill" of the song. The next time I was with him in San Pedro, as I entered his apartment, "Love is a Many Splendored Thing," was playing on his stereo. I rushed into his arms and ever since this has been, "our song."

The wedding was beautiful and all present had a good time; white and black. We were blessed with many wishes for our happiness. We had asked for no gifts, but we received enough money to make our honeymoon a rich experience.

Chapter 4

My Name is Mary Ivy Fox

A few weeks after the wedding, we left for Paris. The first night we enjoyed the show at the Moulin Rouge. We saw the Opera House, Montmartre and Notre Dane, and ate at a sidewalk café. We went out to the Versailles Palace and took a ride on the Seine River; and, of course, we went up the Eiffel Tower. We also saw the Louvre Museum, but did not have time to go in.

Then we took a high-speed train, first class to Avignon. There we saw the bridge that goes half way across a river, visited a winery that had very short grapevines and made wine for the Pope. For many years, a Pope had lived in Avignon.

We then went by bus to Nimes, along the way seeing a 2,000-year-old Roman aqueduct, still amazingly well preserved. In Nimes, we learned how our word, "denim" originated. It literally means "from Nimes" (De Nimes).

We then rode the bus to Nice and along the way went through Arles, where Van Gogh lived and painted. Nice is on the Riviera, but we were disappointed in the beach, we saw not much sand and a lot of rocks.

Then, afterwards, we returned back home after a fabulous honeymoon to be Mrs. Logan Fox.

God has blessed me in this marriage. Logan is a perfect husband, and I could not be happier.

Logan was born to missionary parents in Japan, the second of seven children. In 1935, the family returned to America and Logan got a college education, married and had a child Ramona.

In 1948, he returned to Japan where he spoke the Japanese language. He was able to preach, and with others, establish a Christian school. He was most active in building the college where he was first Dean, and then President.

He came back to America in 1960, with his wife and five children. Here he has taught at Pepperdine and El Camino Colleges, retiring in 1987, the same year I did.

We had decided when we got engaged that we would worry about where to live later. After the wedding, we decided that it would be best for him to move in with me since the house I lived in is paid for and Logan was paying $1,100.00 a month in rent for his apartment. I had to get ready for Logan to move in with me. Finally, on July 9th, four months after the wedding, we became a family.

Our marriage has been a happy time for both of us. We still took our morning walks with our friends at the circle until my knee gave out. We love to listen to music at our happy hour and at bedtime. We play games, work puzzles and watch TV together; I do word puzzles and Logan does crosswords. Logan is a reader and often reads to me; and, we love to travel. Logan had some money from the sale of his home. As a result, we have taken twenty-four trips in the fourteen years we have been married. We have been to Hawaii, Alaska, Japan, England, Ireland, Mexico, Guatemala, Costa Rica, Panama (and the Canal), Germany, France, Croatia, the Greek Islands, Greece, Spain, Egypt, Israel, Holland, Switzerland, Canada, Italy and Turkey.

I thank God for the many blessings He has given me. Letting me live for ninety-six years and blessing me with a loving partner to share the closing years of my life. What a bonus this is!

I thank God for all the good people I have met and loved.

~ Mary Ivy Fox ~

Added Notes

The year 2011, I turned ninety years old and this was a big thing for me. I am the only one of seven children to live to be ninety. My younger brother was eighty-three and my sister, Julia, was still alive. I told Logan that I wanted to celebrate the whole month of May.

First, we cruised up the Pacific Coast with members of the "Fifty + Club" to which we belong, and they celebrated with me as I was crowned. In Victoria, Canada, we visited the beautiful Butchart Gardens and had high tea at the Empress Hotel.

After being home for a few days, we flew to Atlanta where a host of relatives gave me a wonderful celebration. I saw so many nieces and nephews and cousins, some of which I didn't even know.

Returning home to Los Angeles, we had another celebration at the Proud Bird Restaurant. I invited one-hundred guests to enjoy a delicious sit-down meal and lively music.

In October of 2016, at Logan's suggestion, I finally sold the place King put me in. As a bonus, I have some money.

Three practices that have enriched our married life:

One is the happy hour at three o'clock. We both stop doing whatever we were doing and we come together for a glass of wine or a Martini and snacks and music. We relax, reminisce and just enjoy being together.

Another is the weekly dinner out. Every Tuesday we go to one of our favorite restaurants for a treat. It's like being on a date and we experience ourselves differently than our day-to-day selves.

The third is bedtime music. We choose a disc from our collection and play it as we go to sleep. We have Frank Sinatra, Dean Martin, the Ink Spots, the Platters, Nat King Cole, and others.

*"God is good all the time;
all the time God is good."*

Dr. and Mrs. Logan Fox

www.ingramcontent.com/pod-product-compliance
Lightning Source LLC
Chambersburg PA
CBHW070749050426
42449CB00010B/2392